ROCKABILLY

MIKE WILSON

ROCKABILLY

TRANSLATED FROM THE SPANISH
BY JORDAN LEE SCHNEE

DIAPHANES

Only the lonely
Know the way I feel tonight
Only the lonely
Know this feelin' ain't right

Roy Orbison

ROCKABILLY

Rockabilly started digging late one spring night with a rusty shovel in his backyard.

Everything had begun a few hours earlier. It was getting late; the lights in the neighborhood were starting to come on, and the red stain on the horizon was growing faint. In some houses TVs flickered. In others, families gathered around the dinner table. But Rockabilly had no family, no TV. He was in the living room, under a weak light bulb, kneeling on a pile of old newspapers, his greasy fingers working to take apart a transmission he had picked up at the junk yard. He wiped a hand across his forehead, replacing the sweat with a black smudge. Satisfied, he went into the bathroom. As he was soaping up his arms in an unsuccessful attempt to remove the dark streaks that clung to his skin, something fell from the sky.

First he heard a high whistling sound, then a dull thump on the roof, an explosion, and then muted impact in the backyard. Rockabilly ran out of the bathroom. The edge of the roof was in flames, the gutter hanging precariously. Without panicking, he got the extinguisher he kept in the kitchen and put out the fire. Once the smoke had cleared, Rockabilly inspected the damage. Besides a charred semi-circle, the only evidence that something had fallen from the heavens was a hole the size of a coin through which a single star shone.

Rockabilly put down the extinguisher and stood looking at his backyard. He scratched his chin, contemplating the small domestic apocalypse. An incandescent mist was floating on the grass; the earth was gashed open, and scraps of vegetation were lying around the yard. He took a few steps towards the center of the furrow, following the path of one of the tendrils of fog. As he advanced, the movement of his legs dispelled the mist, allowing him to see for an instant what was under the surface. He continued cautiously until he came upon a hole in the yard. Rockabilly knelt down and could see the misty contours of a small crater. The fog was flowing down into it.

He stood there for a few minutes, not knowing what to do. He thought about calling someone. The fire department, the police—anyone. But he discarded the idea. Rockabilly had a criminal record, and he preferred to keep a low profile. Anyway, everything seemed to be under control. The fire was out, the roof wasn't about to fall down, and the yard ... Who the hell cared about the yard? Besides, he was tired. He hadn't slept the night before, and he didn't want to deal with the authorities. Rubbing his eyes, he decided to take care of the mess in the morning. Without looking back, he lit a cigarette and lay down on the sofa.

Rockabilly had moved in four years ago, but he hadn't found the time or the need to buy a bed. In fact, besides a couple of folding chairs, a small table, and a tattered sofa, the house had no furniture. Instead, there were countless pieces of junk all over the place. Screws, spark plugs, shock absorbers, dismantled motors, vintage tires, and rusted tail pipes. The mere idea of having to organize this chaos exhausted him. Still, even though he was dog tired, he couldn't calm down. He felt restless. He couldn't stop thinking about the crater, how it could be a rock from outer space, a meteorite or something like that. He remembered an article he had read once on one of the scraps of newspaper covering the floor. Something about the commemoration of the 40th anniversary of man's walking on the moon. It said that the moon rocks they had brought back were worth millions of dollars. Rockabilly couldn't get the figure out of his mind. The possibility that an extraordinary rock was now buried in his yard kept him awake. He was already imagining selling the meteorite for thousands of dollars and finally being able to buy the parts he needed for his low-rider.

He swept aside the covers, put on his jeans, went to the garage, and got the shovel.

The night was warm, and it was hard work. The thing was lodged down deeper than Rockabilly had thought. Drops of sweat ran down his face, and his shirt stuck to his skin. He took it off, and kept digging energetically. He didn't doubt that with every huff, every grunt he was nearing his prize.

While Rockabilly kept shoveling, without him suspecting her presence, she watched him from a dark window. Her shining eyes revealed the same ardor that possessed Rockabilly. She spied on her neighbor's efforts from the safety of her home—how the muscles in his arms and torso contracted, how the tattoo of the pin-up girl that covered his back seemed to dance in the light of the full moon.

SUICIDE GIRL

I'm in my room, looking at myself in the mirror, trying
to see myself in a way that doesn't disgust me. I scrutinize my face, looking for an angle, a shadow, an expression, anything. I know I'm not ugly. I know how the
boys at my high school look at me. I guess they think
I'm hot, but right now I can't convince myself. I open a
drawer and take out my make-up. Dark eye shadow, and
the reddest lipstick I have. I start putting it on. I want
to look like her. I put up my hair, I grab the eyeliner, I
draw a beauty mark on my cheek and a tattoo on my
arm. It's the silhouette of a woman. I picture her posing
in an old-fashioned bathing suit. Now I look better. I'm
about to step away from my reflection when a radiant
glow fills the room. I feel the light, its weight, like it was
hitting me. It penetrates my whole body, it goes through
me, it transforms me. It all happens in a matter of seconds. The light is followed by a bang. Something, dirt,
splatters against the window. My lizard hides behind
a rock. Then it gets dark. Silence descends again over
the neighborhood, and a few moments later the crickets
restart their chirping, like they can't hold their breath
any longer.

I stick my head out of the window and see my neighbor with a fire extinguisher, putting out a small blaze
at one end of his roof. I bite my lip and sigh. I always
do this when I see Rockabilly. I can't help it. I think I
spend more time spying on him than anything else. I

know his routine. He goes out to look at the sky when the sun is setting, and doesn't reappear until early in the morning, before I go to school. Mom gets really angry when she catches me watching him. She tells me that a 15-year-old girl shouldn't be going around spying on people. Especially a greaser like Rockabilly with his junk cars, his hell-raising motorcycles, his pornographic tattoos, and who knows what else. Oh yeah, and that she is worried that a girl my age is so clearly turned on by looking at a man who's over 30. She says I'm playing with fire.

Rockabilly has left the yard. I throw myself down on the bed and shut my eyes. I hate my room, I'm sick of the pink walls. They haven't changed since I was seven. Another one of Mom's whims. Pink walls, pink drapes, pink closet, pink dresser, pink hell. My only "luxury" is Chuck, my lizard. The day I got him was a dark day for Mom. She hates him. She thinks he's a creature that harbors god-only-knows-what diseases. When she told me that, I fell in love with Chuck. I went to the pet store and bought him everything he needed. Now he lives in a terrarium on my desk. It's furnished with a couple of smooth rocks, sand, a dry stick, and a heat lamp. Reptiles need warmth, or else they get stiff.

I hear him scratching. I open one eye. Chuck is staring at me, his neck stretched out, his front legs extended and planted on the ground. Something's wrong, he seems agitated. That strange light must have scared him. I lie still, not doing anything. Chuck stretches out even further, and his tongue comes out. I get up from the bed, and he goes berserk. He gets up on his haunches, and his little claws start scratching at the terrarium's glass. I go over, and he gets even more agitated.

What's wrong, Chuck?

He doesn't stop staring at me, but when I get closer I realize that his miniature eyes aren't looking at mine.

They are fixed on my body, on my breasts. I look down and see that the left side of my pajama top has a wet circle.

One of my nipples is oozing milk.

BABYFACE

My head is heavy, it's hard to open my eyes, my body is lying motionless on my La-Z-Boy armchair. My hands, bars of lead, won't respond. I manage to half-open my eyes; I see faded shadows. I'm able to unstick one of my arms, and I start feeling my face, exploring my cycloptic skull. Slowly I rediscover the dimensions of my head. Huge, round, soft. I run my fingers through the silken fuzz that barely covers the crest of my scalp and inhale deeply a couple of times, trying to get oxygen. I grope around my thigh until I find the catheter, pull the device and feel how it releases from my bladder. There is a burning sensation as it slides out of my penis. I wet myself slightly. My tongue is dry; I forgot to take out my dentures. My gums hurt. I start breathing again, close my eyes. I find the chair's lever and raise up, then wait for gravity to take care of draining the fluids that have built up in my head. It hurts like my stomach is tearing at my brain. Slowly, my senses sharpen. My vision is restored; I recover movement in my legs and other arm. I wipe the drool from my chin, and I'm about to stretch out my hand to turn on the lamp; when a brightness invades the living room. I reach up with my forearm to shield my eyes, but before I can cover them; the radiant light disappears. I want to go and see what's going on, but my body still wont allow that. I'll have to wait a little longer.

I don't know how much time has passed, I think I dropped off again. I hear a sharp, repetitive noise. It's coming from my neighbor's house. I get up, my bathrobe is open, I'm swaying slightly and stabilize myself against the wall. I head for the window that looks onto the yard. I see my reflection in the window, and my jaw twitches. I still can't get used to my appearance. My body swollen, hulking—a dense, rounded bulge. My yellowy skin, and my head ... I turn away. The kids from around the corner are right: I'm a grotesque Gerber. A freak.

Three years ago, my body started to deteriorate. My head grew and swelled, my skull too. My teeth fell out, and my hair. A slight fuzz took its place. My eyes and ears got bigger. At first the doctors didn't know what it was. They published articles, took photographs. They examined me, took measurements. Nothing, until one day a paleovirologist discovered I was infected with a virus that was thought to be extinct. It causes a disease called FCI, facial-cranial infantilism. The face in the reflection that returns my gaze is a 40-year-old baby's.

I rest my head against the glass and block out the light with my hands so I can see what's happening in the darkness of the neighboring yard. It's difficult to see, but my eyes adjust to the low light. Rockabilly's sweaty torso is shining in the moonlight as he feverishly digs. The hole is up to his knees. The rhythmic movement of his labor makes the tattoo covering his back seem to come alive. I close my bathrobe. I watch him a little longer, trying to figure out what he's looking for, what he's planning. I remember the light, that brightness. My head is starting to hurt in this position, and I pull away from the window. I feel how the skin on my forehead unsticks from the glass, leaving a foggy mark in its place. There's something strange there—it's hard to focus my vision. I manage to right before the steamy print vanishes. I see translucent letters, written in the sweat. They shrink, like an anorexic code about to expire. The word evaporates, and the glass returns to transparency. Still, when I close my eyes I can see the letters. They are clear, neat, meticulous.

K I L L

BONES

That light did something to me. My head is full of things, ideas, words. I think. I can't stop panting, it's exhausting, it feels like a bee has gotten into my head. It won't stop buzzing. It's got something to do with the neighbor. I scratch, scratch, scratch. I don't know why, but since I saw that light, my head has been talking to me. Every time I do something, it instructs me. I scratch. It's bested me. I can't fight it. I walk towards the fence. I go up to it. I know that the neighbor is in his yard. I can smell his butt. I smell it. It's about 25 feet away. I smell his butt. I know the neighborhood's butts. I know when they go out into their yards. Right now, Rocka-billy's butt is in its yard. I scratch, scratch. I get closer to the fence. I get up onto my hind paws. I see Rockabilly's butt. His butt is digging. I know how to dig. It's one of the things I do. Dig, shit, eat, sleep, dig, scratch, dig. I also smell the other neighbor's butt too—Babyface's, but it's further away, indoors. I smell it anyways. It smells like baby powder. I scratch, scratch. Suicide Girl is fur-ther away. I smell her butt and milk too. I want milk. I want milk. I want milk. It makes me want to bark. I do my hungry bark. I do it 18 times: Hungry! Hungry! Hun-gry! Hungry! ... and on and on until I'm satisfied. I look again at the pit Rockabilly's butt is digging. Something is bothering me. I know how to dig. I know how to dig, but it doesn't turn out like that. It's embarrassing. I want to dig like that. I want his hole. I want to go inside and turn around six times and lie down. I hate Rockabilly's butt. It's humiliating me. I want Rockabilly's butt's hole. I should hatch a plan. I scratch, scratch. I don't know how to hatch plans. I need to get my head to tell me how to plan. I raise my snout again. I see the painted skin, the woman on Rockabilly's butt's back. She smells different. She looks at me, and she smells different. Her eyes speak to me. They offer me what I desire. They tell me how to get it. I don't know how, but I know I should do it.

There's a growl in my chest.

SUICIDE GIRL

I see him digging. I turn off the lights in my room, and I open the window so I can watch him better. She's with him. She's always with him. Beautiful, seductive, eternal. He buries the spade forcefully, and she reacts, swaying her hips as if she were trying to shake off the drops of sweat sliding down Rockabilly's back. I see the pin-up's voluptuous chest, and I remember my own breast. It's swelling up bigger and bigger. It hurts. My chest looks strangely lopsided. The milk keeps coming out of my left nipple. I covered it with a sanitary pad, but that was no use—the liquid soaked through in no time. I'm afraid. I feel like telling Mom. Maybe she will know what's wrong. It could be a remnant of puberty, I don't know, something hormonal. She probably knows. But I change my mind. I'm sure she's going to think the worst, like I'm pregnant or something. Mom is sure I'm a little slut. Once I heard her talking to one of her friends who comes over once in a while. I was in the hallway; they were in the kitchen. Mom told her that she had given up on me. That she had a daughter who dressed like a skank, and she was sure I had gone all the way with more than one guy. Since that day, I haven't stopped hating her. I don't care what she thinks of me, and I'm not even going to bother telling her that I'm still a virgin, that I'm afraid of sex. It's not like I don't want to. Sometimes I even get obsessed with thinking about it. But I prefer imagining it when I'm alone ... The other way seems painful. Like monkeys. I don't know.

A sharp pain takes me by surprise. I suppress a scream. I can't take it anymore; it hurts. My top is soaked through. I admire Rockabilly for another few seconds and close the window. As I massage myself, I remember something that might soothe the pain. Mom still has an electric breast-pump from when I was a baby. I find it in a drawer in the bathroom, still in its original box. I go back to my room, close the door, read the instructions, and plug in the machine. It still works. I take off my pajama top. Chuck goes wild, hopping around, scratching at the glass, battering his head against the walls. It's disturbing. I cover the terrarium with a blanket. I can still hear his scrabbling. I ignore it. I look at my naked breasts, the left one is almost double the size of the right. I apply the suction cup and press it down, following the instructions. With my other hand I squeeze, like I'm juicing an orange. I'm not sure if I'm doing it right, but I have no idea what else to do. I turn on the machine, which starts humming, and I feel how the suction pulls at my breast. There's a burning sensation in my nipple. Suddenly, the milk starts coming out in spurts, not a continuous stream. Spurt, pause, spurt, pause, spurt. I want to laugh. After about ten minutes I feel much better. The swelling in my left breast is gone, and the little recipient that connects to the pump is almost full. The milk looks creamy, delicious. The bottle is warm, and for a second I want to take a taste, but I reconsider and pucker in disgust.

Chuck is still scrabbling around. I feel bad and uncover him. He sees the bottle of milk in my hand and freezes, his little eyes glued on the creamy liquid. I don't know why, but I understand exactly what I have to do. I stick my arm into the terrarium and move my hand towards the shallow bowl to fill it with milk, but I don't get that far. Chuck jumps up and bites my wrist. I drop the bottle and pull my hand back. I'm bleeding. I bring the wound to my lips. He's never attacked me before. I look at him in surprise. Chuck doesn't seem to be aware of me, his head is bent down, and he's desperately drinking the spilled milk. I watch him for a little while. I know that reptiles aren't capable of facial expressions, but I swear to God that on Chuck's face is an expression of sinister euphoria ... Insatiable.

ROCKABILLY

It's hard for him to get the shovel into the ground. The heat of the impact crystallized the soil. It crunches like glass cracking. Rockabilly needs several minutes to break through the upper crust of the crater. Slowly, the earth starts to soften, changing from a rigid shell to sandy mud.

Rockabilly smiles as he throws the dirt over his shoulder. The neighborhood is quiet; the spade disappears into the dark silt. He doesn't get distracted; he continues to work steadily. A mysterious will has taken hold of him. He feels his arms getting tired, the muscles in his back burning, but he can't to stop the hunt, nor does he want to. A drop of sweat travels down his vertebrae. The hot fluid caresses the pin-up's stomach, and crosses her as if cutting her in half. The droplet leaves a lustrous trail, a cauterizing wire. As he digs, he could swear he hears the hiss of it evaporating.

He remembers that day with a heavy heart. It's been months since Rockabilly has thought about that sweltering afternoon. He had managed to push it out of his thoughts. And now here it comes again. The abandoned house in the suburbs where they sold crystal meth and repaired choppers. In a dirty bathroom a woman who did tattoos was waiting. She wore a flower-print house coat and had unicorn hair clips. She was made up like a perfume saleswoman, had on brown tights, and boasted pure skin. Unblemished, not even a single line of ink. She said her name was Penny. She was wearing a ring with an enormous diamond. Her breath smelled of coffee and cigarettes. The rest of her body smelled like hairspray.

Rockabilly pulled up his shirt, exposing his back. A Johnny Cash song was sailing through the house. Penny was chewing gum. She turned on the tattoo gun; the machine buzzed. She brought it towards his skin.

Are you sure?

Yes.

This is gonna hurt ... A lot.

BABYFACE

I tie my bathrobe and go out into the front yard. The street is dark; on the corner there's a stop sign, and an anemic light is coming down off a lamppost. Across the street, a voluptuous old oak tree hangs over the sidewalk as if it were waiting for some distracted pedestrian. Prey. Meat to feed the night. The sky is cloudless; a flock of nocturnal birds eclipses the stars, flying by silently. I prefer to go out like this, late, when everyone else has retreated into their suburban caves. I can walk easily, without having to deal with bullshit from the kids. Fucking kids. I adjust my slippers and go onto the sidewalk. I walk. This is part of my ritual, doing a couple of laps around the block, strolling in the moonlight, listening to my slippers scrape against the cement slabs. I forget my monstrosity, the weight of my head, the fragility of my body. I go at my own pace. Slowly, stopping when I need to breathe a little extra. I feel good. Alive.

I go by Rockabilly's house. I can hear him digging. I remember the message on the glass. I close my eyes and can see it again. What's strange is that I'm not so worried about this thing with the window, the letters. What makes me nervous is that since that moment I've rehearsed the actions in my mind more than once. I've been thinking about how I would kill him. Strangulation. A shot to the head. A knife to the kidney. Or maybe something more sophisticated like arsenic, or a simulated accident or suicide.

I go by his house a couple more times.

What's weird is that I barely know him. I don't have any reason at all to hate him. In fact, I don't hate him. I even think I might like him. Him and that beautiful woman that graces his back. Still, when I imagine his murder I have no doubt in my mind that I'm capable of doing it without the least hesitation.

The neighbor's dog has started barking. I go around the corner and pass the girl's house. The one that haunts my dreams. She dresses like a teenage version of Rockabilly's tattoo. Sometimes I watch her from my house, but I hate myself for doing it; I feel like a pedophile. I feel like I'm degrading myself on the inside, that I'm becoming the monstrosity that my body projects. I need to keep a core of goodness; I can't be that man. The man who lives in a quiet suburb and stalks young girls—a vile man. I close my eyes and soothe my urges by thinking of Rockabilly's pin-up, but inevitably her seductive form transforms into my teenage neighbor.

I adjust the bathrobe and keep going. I walk in circles, well, actually in squares, passing by my neighbor's houses until I can't take it anymore. The irrefutable idea once again takes over my mind. I seize hold of it, playing out Rockabilly's death again and again. My indifference to the act no longer seems strange to me; just the opposite, now I find it comforting. I close my eyes again and see myself strangling him with my own two hands. I am in the pit he has dug, kneeling on top of him, crushing his trachea. I see his body convulsing, see my shoulders and back flexing, him digging his nails into my forearms. I want to see it all, see how Rockabilly's face contorts, how he goes pale. I want to be the first one to appreciate the blush of blue that tints his features. But no matter how hard I try, my efforts fail. I can't see his face.

My fucking head is blocking my view.

BONES

My tongue is dry. I drink some pool water. I scratch, scratch. I get the voice in my head under control. She's helping me. The tattoo woman. The one who dances on Rockabilly's butt's back. She arranges the words that I'm hearing in my head. Now I can sort the ideas, the urges. She helps me to plan. She invites me over to the hole that Rockabilly's butt is digging. She asks for my help in freeing her from the the prison of flesh, saying the hole will be mine if I do what she asks. I scratch, scratch. The other neighbor's butt—Babyface's—has started moving. It's not in its house anymore. It's gone out for its night time stroll. It gets close to the front yard. I smell it. I hear the scrape of its slippers. I bark eight times. It's a bark that I use to say that I am paying attention. Every yelp ends in a soft growl. I chew my tail a little. The tattoo woman's voice is telling me something. That I should go out into the street, that a green van is going to go by soon, and I should chase it. I like chasing cars. It's one of the things I do well. Scratch, eat, shit, bark, dig, chase cars. She tells me the people who are going to help me will be in the car. That they will be on my side, be my allies. I hope there's a girl dog in the group. I look at the smoothness of my crotch. I smell the little hairy part and I growl. My owner had me neutered when I was a puppy, but I still want a girl dog. I let out an unintentional bark. Impulsive, wimpy, high. The tattoo woman interrupts my reverie, telling me to hurry up—it's getting closer. I go by the side of the house and out to the sidewalk. Here it comes. I can see the van's lights and feel the motor's rumble. I give a couple of preparatory barks. The van goes past me and I go after it like a shot. I run and bark. I run and bark like a rabid dog. I don't know what this bark means; it's the one that I always bark when I chase cars. I just don't ask myself.

SUICIDE GIRL

Chuck's sleeping. He looks weird. He's lying on his back, his stomach swollen. It's funny, he's got a milk moustache. As I'm looking at him, I get the urge to smoke. I check inside the boot where I hide a pack and confirm what I had suspected. It's empty. I know that Mom has some, but she always keeps her cigarettes on her, and if she caught me the bitch would ground me for a month. The other thing is, I don't want her to see me. I feel how my breast is filling up again, and I don't have the least fucking idea how to explain what's going on. I need to smoke, to get rid of this disgusting feeling, calm down a bit. I stick my head out of the window, Rockabilly is still there, digging. I know he smokes some weird filterless brand. I want to talk to him, but I wouldn't dare. Especially in this state. I feel like a mutant. A circus freak. The girllady with the lactating breast.

I go down to the living room, noiselessly. Mom is in her room. I see the light from the TV. The theme music from the Osmonds is playing. Mom always leaves the keys to the van hanging in the kitchen. I cautiously go out the front door and see the van parked in the garage's entrance. I put the clutch in neutral, and the van moves silently, rolling down slowly until reaching the asphalt. I bite my lip and turn on the motor. I stay like that a little while, watching Mom's lit window, waiting for any movement, any shadow, but there's nothing. I start breathing again and accelerate. The Wal-Mart is close, eight or nine blocks away, which will let me get back before she realizes I've left. I hope Junior's working. He always sells me cigarettes without asking for ID. I turn on the radio. Mom left the Carpenters in the cassette deck. I hate the Carpenters... I want to hate them. Sometimes, when I'm alone, and a song of theirs comes the radio, I turn it up. I hate that they make me feel good. I hate that I like them so much.

Before I get to the corner, I see a shadow crossing the street. It's close. I'm almost on top of it. I step on the brakes with both feet; the wheels shriek. A few windows light up. I scream and get out of the car, furious. It's that freak, the old Gerber. He's standing there in the middle of the lane, his huge head looking at me with big; blue; beautiful eyes. The silky wisps of hair on his skin undulate in the breeze.

I'm gonna kill you!

...

Did you hear me, you fucking geezer?

Sorry, I was...

My anger dissipates; there is something in his eyes, in his stooping posture, that makes me feel sorry. I regret having yelled at him.

Are you okay, sir?

Yeah.

Please take care. There might be an accident if you walk around like that.

Yes. I know. I'll be more careful.

Now that I've calmed down a bit, I realize he's wearing nothing but a bathrobe and a pair of slippers. He seems distracted. He doesn't lift his gaze, like he was afraid to look me in the eyes.

Sir, I'm your neighbor. Do you want me to bring you back home?

No, thank you.

Do you need me to bring you somewhere? Are you lost?

I want a Pepsi.

I fall silent for a minute, watching him, trying to decide what to do with him. I think he's no harm he has something innocent about him. And if Junior isn't on, maybe Gerber can buy the cigarettes for me. I talk to him slowly, for some reason, I think if I talk quickly he won't be able to understand.

I'm going to Wal-Mart. Do you want to come with me? They have a lot of Pepsi. Cans and cans and cans. A whole aisle.

Without answering, he gets into the car and settles into the passenger seat. I take the wheel and watch him. He's looking straight ahead unblinkingly. I've never seen him from this close. In the neighborhood there's always talk of him. The bigheaded monster. The gross Gerber. But now that I get a good look at him, he has something, I don't know, something lovely. His round shining eyes. His smooth skin. The soft hair that rests on his head. Plus he smells really good. As I'm admiring him, I feel my nipple starts dripping again. I want to take him in my arms, kiss his cheek, tickle him, caressing his body so he'll suckle. I take the wheel again. I turn up the cassette and wrinkle my nose in disgust. I should feel disgusted. I want to feel disgusted. It's a sick picture. I guiltily look at his baby head guiltily,. I feel like a pedophile.

I look away, step on the gas, and we head off for Wal-Mart. As we move forward, I hear the sweet melody of the Carpenters and the wild barking of a dog chasing us.

BABYFACE

She has a little pin-up drawn on her arm, like a miniature tribute to Rockabilly's ink. We go into the Wal-Mart. I let her go in first and watch how she walks. Her tight body, her put-up hair. She doesn't look like a 15-year-old girl. I adjust my bathrobe and look away. I'm not that man, I tell myself. The fluorescent lights in the store make me feel depressed. Copacabana by Barry Manilow is coming down from the Walmartian heights. She stops in the soda aisle and looks at me. I don't know if I'm imagining it, but it seems like one of her breasts is larger than the other. I think she caught me looking at her; she's blushing. Something about it is confusing—there's no anger in her expression. She's looking at me in a way that I can't really place.

Here are the Pepsis. In cans, in glass bottles, in plastic. Diet, Cherry, Vanilla. It's all here.

I lower my gaze.

Thanks. I like how Pepsi tastes out of little glass bottles. It's even more delicious.

She smiles and tells me not to go too far from this aisle, that she'll be right back. She needs to see if a friend of hers is working. I can't help checking out her legs while she walks to aisle eight.

I'm tired. The back of my neck hurts. It's my head; I need to rest it on something. In aisle six they sell gardening tools. I come across some clay pots that are hanging from ropes and find one without a plant that's the right size hanging around the height of my chest. I stick my face into it and support my head in the container. The relief is immediate. It's cool inside the pot and damp smelling. At the bottom there are three little holes punched out, which let a little light in. I can see my slippered feet through them.

I feel someone touch my shoulder and leave their hand resting on my back. It's her. Her shoes come up to me through the little holes in the pot.

Are you okay?

I say that I am, but I don't think she hears me. I pull my head out of the pot and smile at her. She returns the smile. Her hand is still on my shoulder.

Can you do me a favor?

I nod yes.

But you need to promise me you won't tell my Mom ... Promise?

I promise.

My friend Junior isn't working right now and he always lets me buy cigarettes ... but he's not here. Get it?

She puts on a suffering pout. She's still looking at me in that same way, with an intensity that at once both excites and embarrasses me.

I'll buy them for you.

Suicide Girl's face lights up and she wraps me in a tight hug. Her body pressed against mine is smooth. It smells so good. I sink my nose into her hair, take a breath, then push her away. I adjust my bathrobe. I don't want to be that man. She blushes again, like she also sensed something off in the air.

The cashier messes up a couple of times when ringing us up. He won't stop staring at my head. She gives me money, and I pay for the pack of cigarettes and the little bottle of Pepsi. We go out of the Wal-Mart in silence. I don't know what time it is, but it must be past midnight. The van is the only car in the parking lot and for some reason there is a huge dog lying on its roof. When it sees us, it gets down and comes over. Everything makes sense. I recognize the dog. It's Bones. A neighbor's pet. He smells my butt, Suicide Girl's too.

I look at her. The silence stretches on. I focus on the tattoo she has drawn on her arm and close my eyes. When I speak, I lift my chin and look into her eyes. I enunciate the words without stuttering or whispering, pronouncing them with determination.

I have to kill Rockabilly.

SUICIDE GIRL

He said something. I didn't hear him clearly. He mumbled it. I think he said I need to swill from your lily. I don't know. He was looking at my chest when he said it. Actually, he's still staring at it. I think he meant my lactation. Lily? I didn't know that expression. He's not as innocent as he looks, I mean if he's capable of suggesting something like that. I don't know why, but I like him. It's perverse; I feel a thrill in my stomach, even though I'm trying to look like I didn't understand. I think about Mom. If she knew I were in the Wal-Mart parking lot this late, smoking while our mutant neighbor was talking to me about my lilies, and at the same time a huge dog was smelling my butt, she would die. I can't stop smiling. It's perfect. Right now, my life is perfect.

Suicide Girl. That's your name, right? I'm Babyface.
Yeah, I know.
He scratches the dog's head.
His name is Bones, he's our neighbor.
Hi, Bones.
Babyface opens the bottle.
Thanks for the Pepsi.
Thanks for the cigarettes.
Hmm.
The deserted parking lot is intimate. Babyface looks at me, and I feel beautiful for the first time in a few days. Like a calendar girl. A few hours ago, my body disgusted me. Now I'm a whole woman ... Someone should film me. Immortalize me in the movies. Make me into

a giantess, a femme fatale, the kind that stretch across B-movie screens. A torn-up dress, lots of skin, lots of ink. A Japanese dragon tattoo wrapping around my leg, its head getting lost between my thighs. A painted woman, a femme dancing on Rockabilly's back.

I still don't want to go back home. The dog gives me an idea. I get onto the roof of the van and lie down face up. I need to enjoy this moment. Babyface stays near the Wal-Mart entrance with Bones. The night is still. Babyface is a statue. Bones too. The only one breaking this crystalline moment is Rockabilly, and he is digging because the sky demands it; and She, beauty itself, clings to his back, accompanying him. For some reason this notion breaks down. It collapses, as if She were refuting it and wanted to show me the error in my thinking. She says, no, it's not like that. Just the opposite. He is accompanying her, he is the flesh affixed to the tattoo, Rockabilly is the one who is the decoration. She is digging. She's the one calling me, the one asking me to go to the window, to admire the man who grows out of her ink. She loves me; she wants me. Now I understand.

From inside the Wal-Mart, there is the murmur of a loudspeaker.

Ten percent discount on all cereal products. There's a spill in aisle twenty. Ask the cashier for your receipt. No returns on Thursday or Sunday. Bodily fluids, including breast milk, can transmit STDs. There's a spill in Chuck's terrarium. Don't forget to ask for coupons on your way out. Thank you for shopping at Wal-Mart and remember, our business is happiness.

ROCKABILLY

As he buries the shovel, Rockabilly is aware of the pin-up girl on his back; in fact, since they engraved her on his skin, she has never been as present as she is right now. He never named her, worrying this would make her more real, that naming her would be an occult act that would awaken the fullness of her terror. He always thought there was some wisdom in having placed her on his back—an invisible place, a terra incognita, a terrain that favored forgetting. But not tonight. Right now she is as present as if they had tattooed her onto his pupils. He feels her, she burns, she exerts power, she flexes him, makes him keep digging. The rhythmic movement of his labor is how she makes Rockabilly dance. They warned him, but he wasn't then able to understand the risk.

That night, in Penny's bathroom, Cash had stopped playing. He had been replaced by the sweet melodic voice of Roy Orbison. The electric needle pierced his skin and slid in a black cold ink. He could feel the icy bile of it twisting in the skin of his back. He could see Penny's concentrated face in a chrome fixture. She was biting her lip while she applied the machine. Drool, colored pink by her gum, was coming out of the sides of her mouth. A thick drop slipped away, until it dropped off her chin. Rockabilly could feel the liquid sliding down his vertebrae until it pooled at the small of his back. He stayed silent, the pink wetness distracting him from the pain inflicted by the needle.

The gun stopped buzzing, and Penny brought her mouth to his ear. She whispered.

The contours of your skin have spoken to me.

Really?

Shh.

...

She is coming out of the surface. At first I wasn't sure what was coming, but the ink is adapting. I see the shadow of a silhouette. She's beautiful. Her eyes took shape first. Black abysses, full of passion, love, perversity, and vengeance.

Is it a woman?

No. It's more than that.

...

Maybe, at first sight, it's a woman, but don't believe that. She will be much more than a decoration. She isn't the voluptuous, undulating female who graces the trucker's arm, not the mermaid on the sailor's chest, not the Hells Angel's concubine. No.

Penny put emphasis on the *no*, and the gum fell out of her mouth. The putty got stuck behind Rockabilly's ear. Without missing a beat, she picked it up and put it back in her mouth.

She dipped the needle in the ink once again and supported her body on Rockabilly's. While she applied the machine with one hand, she caressed his back with the other, outlining the imaginary silhouette with her index finger. Rockabilly understood that Penny wasn't stroking him—she was caressing Her, she was placating Her, trying to control Her so she could finish her work. Penny was getting excited. She was tattooing with her body on top of his. At that moment, Rockabilly started to feel the promised pain, like the lines of ink were sprouting thorns.

BONES

The voice of the drawing on Rockabilly's butt is far off. There's a lot of interference. For me smells are like sounds. I smell something and it's like it speaks to me. Right now a selection of butts are talking to me. Also there's Suicide Girl's milk and the smell of death emanating from the Wal-Mart. The painted woman teaches me how to filter the noise. She tells me that this is called concentrating. Babyface is scratching my head. He's looking at me with interest, and I return his gaze. My tail moves. I've never been able to control that. It just goes on its own. Once I saw a dog with no tail. He had a little stump, but it wagged all the same. Babyface squats down next to me. His groin is yelling at me. I try to block out the racket so I can hear what he's saying. He's talking to me in that voice that people use to talk to animals and little children.

What are you doing over here?

I answer with a whine.

You're the neighbor's dog. I've seen you when I go out walking at night. You live next to Rockabilly's house.

The name rips a series of barks out of me.

Easy, boy, what's wrong? You know Rockabilly?

More barking.

This time I calm myself somewhat, and I spin around a couple of times to try to let him know that I understand what he's saying. He looks at me sideways and sits down.

Good boy, Bones ... Good boy.

Babyface looks away, but keeps scratching my head. I

feel good by his side. He is watching Suicide Girl. He looks sad, yearning for her. I try to understand. I think it's like when I want to mate; it's an insatiable desire. Sometimes there's no solution but to relieve yourself using whatever's around. There's times when almost everything looks attractive. My owner's leg. The neighbor's cat. A cushion, or my owner's daughter's stuffed animal. It used to be worse. Getting neutered lessened the urges, but they always come back, and they always control me. I feel bad seeing the frustrated desire on Babyface's face. He looks like a newborn without his milk. I want to help him. If I could, I would let him borrow the stuffed animal that I use, but for some reason I don't think that would console him. I get closer and whine a little to show him that he can count on my help. He looks at me again and smiles, but his baby-like eyes reveal fear.

You realized, he says to me.

...

The thing is, she's just 15, and I'm an old man ... A sick old man, a mutant. These are humiliating desires; I don't know what I am, but I hate feeling like this.

I give him a tap with my snout and wag my tail. He sits next to me and we stay like that, watching the night, the deserted parking lot, the van with Suicide Girl lying on its roof. A world illuminated by Wal-Mart's radiant lights, the suburban desolation which is at this very moment the center of the universe, the only place that matters, the only space that exists. Three butts, waiting in silence, thinking in unison about Rockabilly's heaving and panting and the will of the painted woman— how She connects us all, how She too is waiting—but not in silence. All three of us hear her at the same time, her voice distilled in our skulls.

Come to me.

SUICIDE GIRL

Back home. I open the door and know I'm in trouble.
I can smell the menthol smoke from Mom's cigarettes.
She's sitting in the armchair in the living room, her
accusing eyes peering at me through a puff of smoke. In
her right hand she has a miniature bottle of whisky. The
kind you find in hotel fridges, on airplanes. On her lap
there's a craft magazine.

Mom ...

She cuts me off with a simple gesture, raising her
arm and pointing at me. I look at the floor, as if I could
find an answer in the carpet's green wool. There's a little
plastic soldier tangled in the fibers. I wish I could shrink
myself and be able to hide next to the toy man, taking
refuge in a world of pea-colored wool.

How dare you go out at this hour, with a face like
a calendar whore. And what's that black shit on your
arm? If you could see yourself, made up like that ... Fake
eyelashes, red lips. Like a streetwalker! And what's with
your breast?

...

You disgust me.

I don't answer. Mom raises the little bottle to her
mouth and empties it, then looks out the window. I take
advantage of the distraction and head for my room. If
I don't get out of here, I don't know what I might be
capable of. Sometimes I'm surprised by the fantasies of
violence that she provokes in me. The most common

involves the telephone cord wrapped around her neck. When she is right about to suffocate, she manages to murmur *forgive me*. I release the cord, and she finally learns how to love me.

When I get close to the door of my room, I lactate again. The drops slide down my skin. I hear a rustling coming from inside. I go in. It's dark, and going forward I feel a sharp pain on the sole of my foot. It hurts so much that I fall to the floor. Something has pierced through the bottom of my shoe and buried itself in my flesh. I find the switch for the bedside lamp and turn it on. My pillows are covered in sand and glass, a bloody piece of which is protruding from my foot. I look up and see Chuck's terrarium has been completely destroyed. I clench my teeth and pull out the piece of glass. A spurt of blood shoots out through the sole of my shoe. I take it off and start admiring the cut. It's deep. I put my thumb in and explore the wound. It hurts, but I like it. It's still bleeding, which scares me a little. While I'm wrapping the injury in a sanitary pad, I hear a scratching. I'm not sure where its coming from.

Chuck? Are you okay, Chuck?

Silence.

Where are you, Chuck? Don't worry, nothing's going to happen to you.

I start going over the room. I limp over to the bed and lift up the mattress. Nothing.

Who did this to you? Was it Mom? It was her, wasn't it? She always hated you—that fucking bitch never loved you. Chuck? Please, where are you?

I'm exhausted. My foot hurts, my chest, my whole body. I look at the alarm clock, it's almost two in the morning. I undress and put on my pajama top. When I collapse onto the bed, the room dissolves into a pink twilight. I think I can hear Rockabilly's shovel ... or Chuck's scratching. I'm not sure which. I close my eyes and She appears behind my eyelids. Her ink bobs up and down, her dance hypnotizing me as she hums a furious melody.

Burn She-Devil, Burn.

BABYFACE

Bones and I are hiding behind the bushes. I'm resting my head on his rump. Through the leaves we can see Rockabilly's silhouette. Bones is nervous. I feel how his muscles tremble beneath the fur.

Easy, boy, easy.

I pet his belly and he calms down a bit.

Rockabilly looks like a machine, his body bending and straightening like a backhoe. The dirt flies out, travelling through the air until it hits the wall of his house. The hole is already as deep as his waist. She is resplendent through the sweat on his back. I distractedly dig my finger into the moist ground under the bush, like I were copying Rockabilly's action but in miniature—burying my fingernails in the earth, excavating among the roots, leaf litter, earthworms and errant snails. I keep going until my entire hand is entombed. Bones comes over to the cavity and sniffs at the small crater I have created. He gets exited, gives me a bark, and starts digging. Worried, I look back at Rockabilly, but he doesn't seem to register our presence. He's completely absorbed. Bones enlarges what I had begun until he has created a pit the size of his head. Suddenly he stops, and he shoots me an assured look. A growl rolls in his chest. He turns around and leaves at a run. For some reason, I know he will come back.

The light in Suicide Girl's room is on. On the way back from the Wal-Mart we listened to songs by the Carpenters. Bones and I got out of the van on the corner where my house is, and she drove off without saying goodbye. Now I can't stop thinking about her. Meeting her has only made it worse. The way she looked at me without caring about my deformity, as if my morbid infantilism only awakened lust within her. The things she said to me. Her precocious pin-up look. I need to see her again. I desert my post and, crouching, approach the lit window. As I go up to it, I see Suicide Girl lying on the bed, her body splayed, asleep. I adjust my bathrobe. I don't think, or try to control myself. I just act. The window has no lock. I slide it up and enter the pink room. It's a mess—clothes thrown all over the place, glass and dirt on the rug. I stand there, next to her bed, watching her sleep. Her chest rises with each breath. The left side of her top is wet, the fabric sticking to her body. I hear a fly buzzing. It's circling around her foot. She has a cut, it's bandaged, but the blood filters through the cotton. I sit down on the carpet, close to her foot, and rest my head on the corner of the mattress. My hands act of their own accord. They undo the sanitary napkin and uncover the foot. The wound is long, still open, still bleeding. I insert my index finger, and Suicide Girl's body shivers. Her breath catches, but she doesn't wake up. As my finger disappears into the cut, I feel disgusting, like an abomination. I don't recognize myself. I want to control myself, but I can't. The tears overflow, I feel the howl coming up my throat. I try to contain it, to push it into the pit of my stomach, but I'm only able to reduce it. My face goes red and contorts, my eyes grow narrow, my mouth stretches. I cover my mouth, but the scream filters through my fingers. It's a mute shriek, a newborn's cry.

Suicide Girl keeps sleeping. My finger explores the wound.

ROCKABILLY

He thinks he might be getting close—the shovel isn't sinking in so easily anymore. And now She lets Rockabilly look away. While his body keeps digging, he looks up and contemplates the constellations. Ever since he was a kid, he has been amazed by the night sky. His dad thought he was fascinated by the stars, but Rockabilly wasn't looking at the celestial bodies. He was letting himself be captivated by the empty spaces between the lights, those little starless patches of space that invited imagining the reaches of shadow, the depth of bottomless darkness.

She is looking upward too. Her eyes observe the celestial pole. Symmetrical eyes, carefully located between Rockabilly's shoulder blades. Penny took hours on each pupil, the needle applying layer after layer of ink until they made deep wounds that bled black.

This is the most important part, she said.

Rockabilly did what he could to keep from screaming, the pain had passed the point of being surface-level—it felt like the tattoo was anchoring itself to his bones, to his vertebrae, to his spinal cord.

I know it hurts; you don't need to hide it. It's the only way. The eyes can't reflect any light, they need to be buried in dark pits. In the abyss where enigma is born.

While she was talking, Rockabilly could feel how the pink drops of saliva fell into the craters dug by Penny's needle.

Hey, are you afraid?

Of what?

Of what I'm doing to you.

Should I be?

I don't know, it depends if you understand or not what it means, bearing Her on your body.

Her?

Yes, Her.

...

She's beautiful, you'll see in a little, She'll be done before the sun comes up.

I didn't know that the tattoo was gonna be so complicated. It's not gonna cost more than we agreed on, right?

No, even though you're getting much more than you asked for, understand?

I don't know.

Everything will become clear. Soon everything will be different.

And if I don't like it? What happens if I regret it?

Let there be no doubt in your mind, the day will come when you're gonna regret it, and you're gonna curse the night you met me.

But didn't you just say I'm getting more than we agreed upon?

Exactly, honey, exactly cause of that. I'm not gonna ask for anything extra, but She ...

Penny let the sentence go unfinished, digging more ink into his back. Rockabilly bit his lip, stifling a scream. He focused on the blood's taste. It was bitter, like a burst pen in his mouth.

SUICIDE GIRL

I wake up. My vision is foggy. I don't get up, trying to see the time on the alarm clock. Little by little, my sight returns. It's 3:33 and still dark outside. The lamp's weak light barely illuminates my room. The window is open, and in the distance I can hear Rockabilly's shovel. I sit up against the headboard. My shirt is unbuttoned. I notice a few streaks on my chest. They're tiny dirty footprints. I recognize them, they're Chuck's. The tracks cross my ribs, leading to my lactating nipple. Chuck fed while I was sleeping. I break into a smile. The discovery makes me happy; it means that he's OK, that Mom didn't kill him.

The bandage has come off my foot. I find the pad on the floor, far from the bed. I check the wound, the cut has stopped bleeding. A black lip of coagulated blood rims the gash. I look at the rest of my foot. Dried blood covers the sole and part of my heel. There's something weird. I get closer to the lamp and see fingerprints, preserved in bloody tracks. Someone was here. They touched me. Mom. She doesn't usually come into my room, especially at this hour, but she was drinking. Probably she won't even remember in the morning. She'll wake up with her fingers stained with blood, and she won't know why. I remember what she did to Chuck's terrarium, and my mouth goes dry. My hatred makes that happen sometimes, when it's intense.

In my dresser drawers I find a handkerchief that I bought last summer. Back then I liked to put my hair up in a bandana, like a worker pin-up. I wrap my foot and sweep up the glass on the carpet with one of my high-school folders. I start looking for Chuck. I check under the bed, I move the furniture, but besides the little footprints on my chest, there's no trace of him. I loose hope. Anger again gets the better of me, I take one of my red patent leather shoes and throw it. It flies out of the window, which I immediately regret. I had to save up for six months to buy those. I go over to the window to see if I can find it, but the patio is full of bushes, and it's dark out, so I can hardly see a thing. I stay there, watching Rockabilly's silhouette. I can only see him from the waist up, the rest of his body disappearing into the hole. At times, the light spilling in from the street catches him, and his body shines. It never lasts for more than a second, but it lets me see his muscles flexing, the drops of sweat bathing his back, while She is lit up in full. Her curves, firm thighs, voluptuous breasts, full lips, deep eyes. I feel her watching me and hear the tune in my head again. She repeats her whisper. *Burn She-Devil, Burn.* It starts to make sense. Let her burn, the goddamn bitch, let her burn.

What are you doing up?

I turn around, Mom's form darkens the door to my room.

Nothing. I was opening the window. I was hot.

Baby...

What?

You know that I love you, right?

...

I know that sometimes I go too far, and I don't behave like a Mom should. I yell at you and say things that I regret. It's just that I don't understand why you insist on provoking me the way you do.

...

Well, I didn't come to scold you, I just want you to know that I love you. Never forget that.

I won't forget Mom.
Well, go back to bed, it's late.
Okey-dokey.
Good night, sweetie.
Bye Mom.

BONES

I'm carrying a ragdoll in my jaws. I go up to the bush
and see Babyface waiting for me. He's sitting next to the
small hole we dug together. He smells different. I smell
blood. His fingers are stained. I drop the doll, go up to
him and lick at his hand. It tastes like Suicide Girl. I
know this because my senses of smell and taste are con-
nected. Smelling her is tasting her. Sometimes Suicide
Girl bleeds. I howl more than usual when that happens.
Babyface's fingers taste like Suicide Girl's bloody crotch.
He's quiet. Besides scratching my head, he doesn't react.
He's got a lost look on his face. Something flies over our
heads and falls a few yards away from where we are. I
can't resist. I let out a yelp and run off to look for it. I
don't understand why I do it, but the impulse is over-
powering. As I run forward, I raise my snout, the aroma
comes down on the air, and a trail of smell covers me.
The object is also Suicide Girl's, but there's something
more, something I can't place. It doesn't take me long to
find it, lying next to the neighbor's oak tree. I get closer.
It's a shoe. I hear a scratching coming from inside of it.
I bear my fangs and let out a growl. The shoe starts to
shake, something moves in the shadows, I get a little
closer and sniff. I still can't recognize the aroma, it's
strange. A foreign smell, mixed with a trace of Suicide
Girl. I give it a push with my snout, then back away. A little head with miniature eyes sticks out. A forked tongue
snakes out of its scaly mouth. I wag my tail. I like this.
This will help me.

BABYFACE

I keep on sitting for a little while, just thinking about her. I bring my fingers to my nose and inhale. The dog comes back; he's got something in his mouth. I think he runs his tongue over my hand, but I'm not sure. I close my eyes again; I see Suicide Girl, only that she is Her. She's grown up, no longer the miniature version of the pin-up—she's turned into Her. She's in my house, in my living room. She brings her mouth to the window pane and fogs the glass with her breath and traces the four letters with her index finger. She turns and looks at me. I'm lying in my La-Z-Boy armchair, with the catheter inside my penis. She looks at me and smiles. Now she's a teen again. She's wearing a Wal-Mart T-shirt. She comes close. I can't move. My limbs won't respond. She lifts up her skirt and mounts my body.

Bones appears again. He puts a paw on my knee, rousing me from my stupor. He's got something in his mouth, but it isn't what he had before. It's floppy, dripping. I hear the drops falling on the grass, heavy drops. They make little pops when they hit. It's a thick liquid. I can't see very well. I had my eyes closed for too long. My vision adjusts slowly. Bones goes up to the hole that we dug at the foot of the bush and spits out the limp form. I lean over to see it better. My nose wrinkles. It's an animal, a reptile, I think. It looks dead. Its tail has been severed off, and I see marks on it's little neck. I look at Bones. His muzzle is covered in bile. The lizard's cadaver lies at the bottom of the hole, face up. It has a certain anthropomorphic quality to it. It's because of the amputated tail I think. The reptile looks like a splayed man with a swollen stomach. Its pale hands are clenched into fists. I get closer and touch its chest, pressing down with my index finger like I were trying to wake it up. It's cold and a bit moist; it feels like the body is sweating a postmortem oil. I take one of its little claws and open it. The palm, the fingers are white and fragile. It looks like Suicide Girl's delicate hand. I like her hands, her smooth skin, their soft lines, the long fingers … They could be reptilian. I work the joints at the little elbows and knees. I turn the lizard over, looking at its scaly back. Its hide exhibits patterns typical of reptiles, and yet the markings seem somehow artificial. I wet my thumb and try to erase one, and confirm they are anatomical—not just painted-on. The colored scaling forms a pattern, like a tattoo, an undulating design.

Before I'm able to study it more closely, Bones snatches the lizard out of my hand and puts it back in the hole in the ground. He looks at me and whines. Wagging his tail, he touches the dead reptile with a paw.

What's up, Bones? What do you want?

He wines again and pushes at the body with his paw. He looks away, pointing his snout towards Rockabilly and growls while pawing at the lizard again.

I understand, and scratch his head. Bones understands and bares his teeth at me. A ferocious grimace deforms his canine face. It's wild, violent. The growls become aggressive, demonic. He buries his head in the hole and flays the body, ripping it to shreds. When he moves back from the pit, I see the destruction, the devastation. A puddle of innards, appendixes, and a strange white substance. I dip a finger in the liquid and I bring it to my tongue. It tastes like dairy. Milk, cream, maybe yogurt. It doesn't matter, the test-run has been consummated. I get to my feet and watch Rockabilly's silhouette. I see how his torso moves, how it shines, how it displays the ink on his back ... and for a second, among the pin-up's lines, I think I can discern the undulating markings of a scaly back.

ROCKABILLY

What hurts most are his palms. He's been digging for hours. His hands haven't stopped sweating, the metal, the wood vibrating in their grip. He feels his skin coming off. Sores develop, splinters stab into his left hand, while his right falls asleep. He's lost control of his body, like he were an automaton, a zombie with one sole purpose. A being of flesh, blood, and ink operating mechanically, perpetually sinking deeper into the tomb of its own creation. He asks himself what he will find at the bottom of the pit. He's not so sure anymore; it's got to be something more than a simple meteorite. If it isn't, then why all of this, he thinks, then why do I keep on burying the shovel? A slight breeze blows, the air alleviating him. The night is warm, and the wind cools his sweat. The trees and the bushes sway; he imagines waves in the sea. He remembers the week he spent at the coast, face down, in a cabin near the beach. He was recuperating from Penny's tattoo. It wasn't healing like the others he'd had done. The wounds stayed open, the burning unrelenting. He would apply an ice compress, but after a few minutes it would be water. Sometimes, when he fell asleep, a hornet's nest would wake him. He could swear that the lines of ink were wriggling, that they were adjusting to his body. After five days, a huge blister formed. It covered the entire tattoo. He pressed at it. It was a smooth, soft dome full of liquid. When he pressed down on it with his fingers, he could hear the fluid moving. One day, Rockabilly got up and felt how the weight of the blister had moved down to the lower part of the dome. A sort of spinal pregnancy, he thought. He went into the bathroom and looked at his back, holding a small mirror between his body and the mirror mounted on the wall. The blister was bigger and more transparent than he had imagined. It was see-through. The bulge's convex form acted as a lens that magnified the pin-up's face. Then, when he got closer to the mirror, his movement created a wave in the fluid and the image distorted. The pin-up's facets swelled and stretched. Her mouth blossomed, then her nose and eyes grew ... When the eyes expanded, they took up the entire surface of the dome, and the liquid in the blister went black. Now he couldn't see through it, but he felt a tickle inside. The black fluid swirled like there was something in it giving great flicks of its tail. Rockabilly dropped the mirror. Just as the glass broke, his back opened up, and the liquid poured out. He tried to get away, but he slipped on the viscous substance. When he fell, he hit his head on the bathroom sink.

It's about time you woke up.
    ...
    All right. Come on. Open up your eyes. Don't worry, you're OK, you hit your head.
    Penny? What ... What are you doing here?
    I came to see how you're coming along, to see how She's doing, and if the ink's healing all right.
    But ... How?
    The door was open, and I saw the light on. I rang the bell a few times, but you didn't come to the door, so I took the liberty of coming in and I found you sprawled out in the bathroom.
    Uh ... The thing is ... I'm still a little dazed ... Thanks for taking care of me.
    Don't get me wrong—you're nice and all, but I don't care about your well being. She's the one I came to see.

I wanted to see if She has gotten settled. You're gonna start to understand that you decorate Her. You're the flesh that I added to the ink, nothing more. But don't worry, while you were unconscious I was able to get a good look at your back. She's radiant. Gorgeous. More than I had even imagined. And you ... You suit her well.

SUICIDE GIRL

I leave my room. There was something in Mom's words that touched me. It's been years since she has talked to me like that, years since she's said she loved me. When I turned twelve, I stopped being a little girl, and she became distant, stopped being affectionate. It was an abrupt transition. In my own home, I suddenly felt like I was a visitor—barely tolerated and almost always ignored. The year after that, when I got my period, the silences became outright aggression. Mom started talking to me again, but only to humiliate me. The worst thing of all was that she wasn't doing it out of anger or resentment. No, she enjoyed insulting me. It gave her orgasmic pleasure. That's what hurt the most. I got used to the shit she showered upon me, but I could never turn a blind eye to her delighting in the violence. And now, for the first time in more than three years, I was able to perceive a trace of the mother who only exists in my most distant memories—memories that I now hardly ever explore. A mother who didn't hide the love that she felt for her daughter, a dedicated woman, strong, tenacious, always making sure that I was a happy girl. That was what was most important to her, everything else was secondary.

The TV in her room is still on, the sound muted. From the hall, I can see how its blueish glow is flashing like lightning. I stand in the doorway. Mom's sitting up in bed, her back supported by a pile of embroidered throw pillows. She's wearing a quilted bathrobe, and her face is covered in green cream. It's one of those masks—moisturizing or exfoliating or something. The cream changes hue with the colors projected from the screen. She's watching a male fitness show. I stand watching a while. Mom still hasn't noticed I'm here. The men on the show seem fake. Exaggerated private parts, tiny speedos, their entire bodies tanned and oiled up. They parade down a medieval-themed stage, carrying swords and maces as props. While I'm watching the men flex their muscles, my foot starts to hurt. I shift, supporting my weight on the other leg.

Baby, what are you doing here?

I don't know … It's just what you said to me in my room …

Yeah?

Was it true? I mean, it's been so long since you said something like that, that I don't know what to believe.

Her eyes get moist, and tears start sliding down her cheeks, plowing lines through the green mask. She fans herself with her hands, trying to control the emotion.

Baby, come here, please come here.

I approach, still unsure of her sincerity. When I reach the edge of the bed, she takes me in her arms and hugs me. She wraps me in her body, getting the cream on me, wetting me with her tears. She holds on to me tight and breaks into sobs, loosing control, getting fragile and trembling like a scared girl. I waver for a few moments, but finally give in and return the embrace. I do it unconditionally, taking refuge in the warmth of her body.

Forgive me, baby, please forgive me.

I'm not sure of the sincerity of my response, but I tell her yes, and not to worry anymore, that from now on we can start from scratch, rebuilding what was lost so many years ago. She calms down, combing my hair with her fingers. Mom looks exhausted, her eyes close. While she rests, I clean the cream off of her face and give her a kiss on the forehead. She asks me to leave the TV on, she can't fall asleep without it.

When I get back to my room, I see my bed and my eyelids start to get heavy. I lie down, curl into a fetal position, and turn off the light. Just when I am about to give myself up to sleep, a little noise comes in through the window. It's a weak scratching.

Chuck!

I jump out of the bed and stick my head out of the window. It's dark, but right below me I see the gleam of his tiny eyes. One of his little claws is struggling to scratch at the brick wall. I lean out of the window and reach down with my hand to scoop him up off the ground, but when I touch him, I discover that something is wrong. Horribly wrong.

BABYFACE

I feel strong, invincible. I strip off the bathrobe and let
the darkness bathe my body. Bones comes up to me and
gives me a once-over with his snout, sniffing me like I
were a drug. My head feels lighter. I flex my joints, doing
a couple of squats while stretching out my arms. I run
my hands over my belly and explore the rest of my body.
I feel like a hunk. I lean my head back and face the stars,
opening my mouth, spreading it wide like I were going
to swallow the universe. I stay like that a while, breathing deeply, watching a satellite move slowly across the
black sky. While I stand there, with my head tipped back
and my jaw thrust out, I feel myself opening up. I can
feel everything rotating, as if a pillar had come down
from the cosmos, down through my throat until coming
to rest in the base of my pelvis. It takes root in my pubis,
passes through my flesh and empties my lungs. A sweet
flavor spreads through my mouth. I imagine it's full of
caramelized butterflies, their wings covered in powdered
cinnamon. I feel the pillar turn inside of me, purging my
impurities, opening my pores, my pupils, putting me on
my tip-toes. When it lets me go, I fall flat on my face.
A few seconds later, I catch my breath and pick myself
up off the ground. Casting my eyes downward, I look at
my naked body, harboring the secret hope for a miracle.
But my physiognomy hasn't changed, except that now
I have an erection. I still have the anatomy of a giant
baby. Even so, I don't loose momentum. On the inside, I
feel better than ever before, able to do whatever comes

my way—and right now I know what is wanted of me.

I push Bones aside and go out from behind the bush. I can see a grassy pathway between both yards. I see it in my head, an illuminated path glinting in the darkness. The trail illuminates a shining route from the bushes to Rockabilly's pit. I look up, and She shows herself. She unfurls, occupying the entire geography of his back. She's dancing in the moonlight, her body swaying. Her gaze, though, is fixed. It locks onto my chest, like it was sending out hooks that were trying to pierce my skin. I keep my eyes closed, I can see her better like that, see her movements, her gestures, the flourish of her lips, the sway of her breasts. Suddenly, she starts to wave her arms, beckoning me to come closer, telling me that the time has come, that I need to do what was promised.

I'm lying down again, in my ratty easy chair. The window pane materializes; the glass is wet. This time, nobody is with me, but I don't feel like I'm alone. The air is still, it smells like grain. My breath grows short. Something squeaks, the sound is coming from the window pane. I can see how the letters form, as if like a phantom index finger were tracing them. It repeats the letters, again and again, with a dexterity that amazes me. As my mouth splits into a toothless grin, I admire the redu-plicating message, K I L L K I L L K I L L K I L L K I L
L K I L L K I L L K I L L K I L L K I L L K I L L K I L L
K I L L K I L L K I L L K I L L K I L L K I L L K I L L K
I L L K I L L K I L L K I L L K I L L K I L L K I L L K I
L L K I L L K I L L K I L L K I L L K I L L K I L L K I L
L K I L L K I L L K I L L K I L L K I L L K I L L K I L L
K I L L K I L L K I L L K I L L K I L L K I L L K I L L K
I L L K I L L K I L L K I L L K I L L K I L L K I L L K I
L L K I L L K I L L K I L L K I L L K I L L K I L L K I L
L K I L L K I L L K I L L K I L L K I L L K I L L K I L L
K I L L K I L L K I L L K I L L K I L L K I L L K I L L K
I L L K I L L K I L L K I L L K I L L K I L L K I L L K I
L L K I L L K I L L K I L L K I L L K I L L K I L L K I L

```
L K I L L K I L L K I L L K I L L K I L L K I L L K I L L
K I L L K I L L K I L L K I L L K I L L K I L L K I L L K
I L L K I L L K I L L K I L L K I L L K I L L K I L L K I
L L K I L L K I L L K I L L K I L L K I L L K I L L K I L
L K I L L K I L L K I L L K I L L K I L L K I L L K I L L
K I L L K I L L K I L L K I L L K I L L K I L L K I L L K
I L L K I L L K I L L K I L L K I L L K I L L K I L L K I
L L K I L L K I L L K I L L K I L L K I L L K I L L K I L
L K I L L K I L L K I L L K I L L K I L L K I L L K I L L
K I L L K I L L K I L L K I L L K I L L K I L L K I L L K
I L L K I L L K I L L K I L L K I L L K I L L K I L L K I
L L K I L L K I L L K I L L K I L L K I L L K I L L K I L
L K I L L K I L L K I L L K I L L K I L L K I L L K I L L
K I L L K I L L K I L L K I L L K I L L K I L L K I L L K
I L L K I L L K I L L K I L L K I L L K I L L K I L L K I
L K I L L K I L L K I L L K I L L K I L L K I L L K I L L
K I L L K I L L K I L L K I L L K I L L K I L L K I L L K
I L L K I L L K I L L K I L L K I L L K I L L K I L L K I
L L K I L L K I L L K I L L K I L L K I L L K I L L K I L
L K I L L K I L L K I L L K I L L K I L L K I L L K I L L
K I L L K I L L K I L L K I L L K I L L K I L L K I L L K
I L L K I L L K I L L K I L L K I L L K I L L K I L L K I
L L K I L L K I L L K I L L K I L L K I L L K I L L K I L
L K I L L K I L L K I L L K I L L K I L L K I L L K I L L
K I L L K I L L K I L L K I L L K I L L K I L L K I L L K
I L L K I L L K I L L K I L L K I L L K I L L K I L L K I
L L K I L L K I L L K I L L K I L L K I L L K I L L K I L
L K I L L K I L L K I L L K I L L K I L L K I L L K I L L
K I L L K I L L K I L L K I L L K I L L K I L L K I L L K
I L L K I L L K I L L K I L L K I L L K I L L K I L L K I
L L K I L L K I L L K I L L K I L L K I L L K I L L K I L
L K I L L K I L L K I L L K I L L K I L L K I L L K I L L
K I L L K I L L K I L L K I L L K I L L K I L L K I L L K
I L L K I L L K I L L K I L L K I L L K I L L K I L L K I
```

```
L L K I L L K I L L K I L L K I L L K I L L K I L L K I L
L K I L L K I L L K I L L K I L L K I L L K I L L K I L L
K I L L K I L L K I L L K I L L K I L L K I L L K I L L K
I L L K I L L K I L L K I L L K I L L K I L L K I L L K I L
L K I L L K I L L K I L L K I L L K I L L K I L L K I L L
K I L L K I L L K I L L K I L L K I L L K I L L K I L L K
I L L K I L L K I L L K I L L K I L L K I L L K I L L K I
L L K I L L K I L L K I L L K I L L K I L L K I L L K I L
L K I L L K I L L K I L L K I L L K I L L K I L L K I L L
K I L L K I L L K I L L K I L L K I L L K I L L K I L L K
I L L K I L L K I L L K I L L K I L L K I L L K I L L K I
L L K I L L K I L L K I L L K I L L K I L L K I L L K I L
L K I L L K I L L K I L L K I L L K I L L K I L L K I L L
K I L L K I L L K I L L K I L L K I L L K I L L K I L L K
I L L K I L L K I L L K I L L K I L L K I L L K I L L K I
L L K I L L K I L L K I L L K I L L K I L L K I L L K I L
L K I L L K I L L K I L L K I L L K I L L K I L L K I L L
K I L L K I L L K I L L K I L L K I L L K I L L K I L L K
I L L K I L L K I L L K I L L K I L L K I L L K I L L K I
L L K I L L K I L L K I L L K I L L K I L L K I L L K I L
L K I L L K I L L K I L L K I L L K I L L K I L L K I L L
K I L L K I L L K I L L K I L L K I L L K I L L K I L L K
I L L K I L L K I L L K I L L K I L L K I L L K I L L K I
L L K I L L K I L L K I L L K I L L K I L L K I L L K I L
L K I L L K I L L K I L L K I L L K I L L K I L L K I L L
K I L L K I L L K I L L K I L L K I L L K I L L K I L L K
I L L K I L L K I L L K I L L K I L L K I L L K I L L K I
L L K I L L K I L L K I L L K I L L K I L L K I L L K I L
L K I L L K I L L K I L L K I L L K I L L K I L L K I L L
K I L L K I L L K I L L K I L L K I L L K I L L K I L L K
I L L K I L L K I L L K I L L K I L L K I L L K I L L K I
L L K I L L K I L L K I L L K I L L K I L L K I L L K I L
L K I L L K I L L K I L L K I L L K I L L K I L L K I L L
K I L L K I L L K I L L K I L L K I L L K I L L K I L L K
I L L K I L L K I L L K I L L K I L L K I L L K I L L K I
L L K I L L K I L L K I L L K I L L K I L L K I L L K I L
L K I L L K I L L K I L L K I L L K I L L K I L L K I L L
```

KILLKILLKILLKILLKILLKILLKILLK
ILLKILLKILLKILLKILLKILLKILLKI
LLKILLKILLKILLKILLKILLKILLKIL
LKILLKILLKILLKILLKILLKILLKILL
KILLKILLKILLKILLKILLKILLKILLK
ILLKILLKILLKILLKILLKILLKILLKI
LLKILLKILLKILLKILLKILLKILLKIL
LKILLKILLKILLKILLKILLKILLKILL

ROCKABILLY

Rockabilly feels something. It's lurking behind him, but he is unable to turn around; She won't allow it. He must keep digging. The will that impels him is irrefutable. His hands are bleeding. Drops of blood roll down the shovel and splash off with every shovelful he throws. Rockabilly knows someone is watching him, he can feel their presence. She can also see him. He hears a series of murmurs and moans. It's not far away, and still he can't turn around. Rockabilly has the feeling that they're coming from the bushes that connect his yard to his neighbor's, asking himself if it's not the girl who spies on him. He's surprised Suicide Girl watching him on other occasions, but her indiscretion hasn't ever bothered him. In fact, he likes the idea of being the object of a voyeur. But he doubts it's her. The muttering he heard was too low-pitched, not like a teenage girl. It was more like a man's voice.

Rockabilly hears footsteps approaching. The urge to turn around becomes excruciating. He can barely take the feeling. It's like having a huge itch that can't be scratched. Powerless, he returns to the task ahead and again takes refuge in voices from the past.

Penny.

Yes, beautiful?

Why am I tied to the bed?

For your own good, beautiful … For Her own good.

I don't get it.

You still haven't fully healed. She can't be touched. I

can't allow that.

But it itches.

That's good, very good.

Come on, untie me.

No, honey. I already told you, I can't.

Do something, please, Penny, do something, I can't stand it anymore.

Let's see, kiddo, what do you want me to do?

I don't know, you scratch me.

Okay, but gently.

Like that ... That's it. A little higher up ... That's it.

Like this?

Yeah, thanks. Please, don't stop. A little harder.

That I can't do, beautiful. We don't want to hurt Her.

What's that?

What?

There. Your fingers are going inside. What's there?

Here?

Yeah, right there.

Don't worry, it's nothing serious. Those are her eye sockets. They're deep and lovely. If only you could see them. They're getting more beautiful with every minute.

What are you laughing at?

It's nothing. It's just that, when I sunk my fingers into the eyes, She blinked. Her eyelashes are tickling me.

...

Well, honey ... That's it.

Where are you going?

I've already done my part, and now it's time to go home.

Wait. You can't leave me like this.

Yes, beautiful, I'm going to leave you like that. You're a smart man, and pretty strong. I'm sure you'll be able to get yourself out of the ropes.

Are you coming back?

No, honey. You won't see me ever again. And neither will She.

Penny.

Bye, hon.

Penny.

...

Penny?

She wasn't lying. Rockabilly never saw her again. For a while he looked for her. He went to the outskirts of the city to see if he could find her in the abandoned house where he had gotten tattooed. A couple of meth heads answered the door. They were gaunt, their skin covered in ulcers and scabs. As he had expected, they didn't remember anything—not him, not Penny. After a few months, he gave up. The tattoo had healed, and it didn't give any indication of being anything out of the ordinary. In fact, as time passed, Rockabilly became convinced that Penny had drugged him, that his memories of those hazy days had been altered. The pin-up looked like any other tattoo. Of course, his co-workers at the auto body shop said that it looked very real, but they attributed this to Penny's artistic ability, nothing else. But at night, when She haunted his dreams, he knew he was only fooling himself, that things weren't so simple, that She wasn't going to let Rockabilly control her, to reduce her to mere ink. Sometimes, he woke up in a sweat in the middle of the night, with the image of Her dark eyes burning on the inside of his eyelids. He would go into the bathroom and look at her in the mirror. She would keep still, like it was nothing, like she was just a tattoo. He would allow himself to be convinced, laugh a little, then go back to bed.

BONES

He looks like an infant God. His butt doesn't smell at all; he's a transcendental being, beyond the sense of smell. His naked white form lumbers towards Rockabilly. Corpulent. Luminous. It's Babyface in all of his glory. He looks like a sumo wrestler, but without the diaper. Or a naked Buddha who just learned how to walk. It's beautiful. It's thrilling.

I go up the fire escape that comes off of one side of Babyface's house. I reach the roof and get settled beside the chimney. The view is marvelous. I can see it all. Babyface toddling towards the crater and Rockabilly digging unceasingly. I see him in profile. His face is contorted; he's suffering. On the other side of the yard, I can see Suicide Girl, she's standing in her bedroom window. Her shirt is open, and she's clutching something that I can't quite see. Whatever it is, it's dripping, and Suicide Girl is wearing an expression of terror. She's frozen, standing there open-mouthed, unblinking, staring at the dripping thing in her hand. She looks like a wax statue, frozen in time, like she were a teenager in a slasher film, paralyzed just as she was about to get killed. It's exciting, I'm so happy—it's so scenic, everything's happening all at once, and I can watch it without being bothered.

I look up at the moon and do what's needed to complete this moment. I howl. I do it with relish; it comes out of the depths of my belly. My cry scares a flock of sparrows that was sleeping in an oak tree. They fly off, stunned, directionless, as if the tree had burst into birds.

I wag my tail and howl again.

Once I saw something about birds on my owner's TV, that when they leave a tree so suddenly like that, it's an omen, that they're off to catch a ghost. I don't know much about these subjects, except that death is the strongest smell in the whole world. It's sharp and violent, and it assaults me. I can detect it from a long way off. But dogs aren't like vultures; we can't sense it before it happens.

The breeze changes direction. I recognize the smell coming from Suicide Girl's window. The limp lizard dripping in her hand has just died.

She screams.

She screams like hell.

I accompany her with another howl. I jump and circle, excited with the harmony of our song. We're a chorus that penetrates the densest shadows in the night. A few lights come on.

I go back to enjoying the panorama. Babyface continues on his way, knocking down the space that separates him from Rockabilly. His head is raised majestically. Enormous, round. His slight hair waves in the wind like it were an unstable cloud magnetized to his hairy flesh. Suicide Girl is no more to be seen, she's disappeared into the interior of the house. The dead reptile lies at the base of the window. Little by little, its flaccid body empties. Rockabilly keeps digging. Sweating and suffering while the painted woman sways more excitedly than ever. Her throbbing flesh seduces me.

I suck in air for another howl.

SUICIDE GIRL

His intestines are wrapped around my forearm, his abdomen yawns open. Drops of bile are dripping from my elbow. His small form rests in my palm, and through his ripped-open chest I can see his little heart beating weakly. Chuck looks at me and blinks. He blinks a lot. He's lost two claws, and his tail has been amputated. Part of his body is trembling. I can hear a soft puffing. It's coming from one of his lungs, which is pierced.

Chuck ...

A lump forms in my throat. I don't know what to do, what to think. Meanwhile Chuck looks at me, he looks at me like he's asking for help, like he can't take the pain anymore. I bite my lip and start to cry silently. I put my thumb on his little neck.

Forgive me Chuck ... Soon it will all be over.

I dig my finger into the opening and feel the cold tendons of his esophagus. I press down. His little eyes bulge. They stop blinking. His mouth opens, like he were trying to shriek. While my thumb squeezes out the last trace of life that's left in Chuck's body, I scream for him. I cry out in anguish, in anger, in hate. I've never screamed like this, so loud. I hear a dog howling. I lay chuck down on the windowsill and step back.

An intense fury takes hold of me. I look at the smashed terrarium, then I look away. My eyes shoot daggers through the door, down the hallway, into Mom's room. It was her. That fucking bitch did it. It was all a lie. Her words, her love. Mom did it because she knew that it was the only way to hurt me for real. She calculated it all, with sadistic pleasure. She got close to me with words of reconciliation, when really all she wanted was to find Chuck. She didn't even bother to kill him— she left him in agony. At this very moment she's probably laughing, her and those muscled-up pigs on the TV.

I look at my hands. They're covered in guts. Disgusting. I go to the bathroom and wash them, soaping up as far as my elbows. I rinse off and do it again. I do it four times, until my skin starts coming off. I sit down on the toilet lid, with a towel in my hands, counting the floor tiles. There are forty-two. They interlock like a chessboard, olive and cream-colored. In a corner is a pair of my panties from who knows when. I grab them and bring them to my nose. I don't know why, but the smell consoles me. They smell like me, the most intimate and dirty part of me. It's like I were meeting an old friend I hadn't seen since we were kids, far away from modesty and posturing. It was the most honest part of me. It makes me smile.

Without letting go of the underwear, I head for Mom's room. I drag my feet on the colorless carpet, gathering static electricity and shocking the doorknobs on the way. Her door is open, the lights are out, the TV still beaming out a dark glow that invades the hallway. I crouch down and crawl the rest of the way. I feel safe like that, out of reach of the screen's rays.

I hear Her again. I close my eyes and see her dark silhouette. She's dancing and belting:

Burn She-Devil, Burn.

BABYFACE

I wait next to the lip of the crater. The hole goes up to his chest. I think he might know I'm here, but he doesn't turn around or stop. He keeps digging. With each shovelful he moans. It's a lament, a wail. His head is bent over. His arms are covered in soil. They have drops of sweat coming off them that draw black lines all the way down to the small of his back. What's strange is that the mud isn't touching the pin-up girl. She's clean. And while Rockabilly is digging in anguish, She seems calm. She smiles at me. I eye her body. I can no longer distinguish her from Suicide Girl. She's so beautiful; I want to have her, embrace her, belong to her. I remember how she looked at me in Wal-Mart, how she touched my arm, pressing with her fingers, like she wanted to tell me something secret ... Something intimate. I'm no longer embarrassed about what I feel for her; no one has ever looked at me like that before. Life has been a motherfucker to me; it dealt me a loathsome existence. Suicide Girl's improper, precocious, and carnal look is the only thing I possess. It's a precious image, and I keepguard it jealously—but I won't hide it any longer. I dive into the pleasure it causes within me. No one else is able to desire me, to love me, to look at me like that. Just the opposite. People avert their eyes when they see me. Children insult me, they make their jokes; but She does not. In this perfect moment, she watches me. Her curves undulate on Rockabilly's clenched muscles. She doesn't look away, not once. She doesn't even blink.

I kneel down and scoop up a fistful of mud. I rub my fingers across my face, darkening my eye sockets, I grab another fistful and rub my chest and thighs. She looks at me in approval, slowing me down. Her tongue slides out and She wets her lips. I copy Her. She smiles again.

Extending my arms, I stretch my hands towards the stars, and suck in air like I were about to dive into a pool. I close my eyes and jump. From behind my lids, I see the glowing Wal-Mart sign in the distance, it's bright yellow and bathes me in rays of pure happiness. Under it, I see a blonde woman with a petite body. She looks fantastic, chewing gum enthusiastically, pink drool overflowing out of the sides of her mouth. She gestures at me, beckoning me to go into the store. She shows me her teeth, which are perfect, too perfect. I get close; I can smell her breath. It's horrible; it stinks of an electrical fire.

I open my eyes.

My body falls heavily and lands on top of his back.

Rockabilly falls.

Succumbing to the weight of my flesh, he doesn't fight. He lies face down in the mud. I'm almost completely covering him. I think I hear him cough, but besides that, he doesn't give any sign of life. I stay on top of him, resting. The effort has exhausted me. Once in a while, I feel him move a little, as if he were trying to get me settled on his back. After a little while, I get up from the bottom of the pit. Rockabilly is partially sunken, flattened by the impact. He looks like a toy man, formed from a mold. To one side of his body is the shovel, the steel glinting in the moonlight. The wood is covered in dried blood.

Rockabilly starts convulsing. He pulls his face from the mud, gives two heavy coughs, then starts laughing. His face-down, sunken body stays immobile, yet he is still able to lean back his head and roar with laughter. His back trembles. She seems bothered and looks at me in disappointment. I feel embarrassed. Rockabilly's uncorked laughter grows, it emerges from the hole, travels across the yard and goes into the suburb's streets. It rattles in the neighbor's windows and makes a dog bark. It's a sacrilegious laugh. I feel like he's making fun of me, of Her. It makes me angry.

Shut up.

He laughs even louder. I try to cover my ears, but it's no use.

Quiet! Shut up! Shut up! For fuck's sake, shut up!

I go over to his prostrate body and give him a kick in the ribs. Rockabilly wavers for a few seconds, as if he were considering what to do next. Then without saying a word, he lets his face fall back down in the muck. He lies like that, still as a corpse waiting for burial. Minutes go by. I sit in one corner of the hole, supporting my head on the earth and stretching out my legs. Rockabilly tenses up. It seems like he's watching something in the depths of the mud. I am about to shake him, when his face reappears. He looks different. He's out of breath, but his gasps don't take long to transform into guffaws. I'm confused. The anger returns. I get to my feet and approach him, but before I can give him another kick, he says something. It's barely a whisper. His speech is rough, but he is clearly euphoric. He looks at me with a fond expression. There's affection in his tone of voice.

If you could only see, he tells me.

...

It's that I didn't know ... I didn't know ... There are no words, he tells me.

...

He gestures at the depression his face just made. His eyes are out of orbit, and he's wearing a delirious smile. It's honest, authentic.

Do you get it? It's there ... Right there! I found it! I didn't have a clue ... Nobody could've imagined, nobody could've predicted this.

...

He looses control again and laughs with abandon, but this time I can see something different in his eyes, something that makes me worry. Distress that I hadn't detected before. This time, his mouth laughs alone. His eyes filling up with tears, he looks at me like he was trying to communicate something ineffable.

Please, he begs. Please, hurry up ... Hurry ...

Suddenly, he turns over and plunges his face back into the mud. I can't hear him anymore, but I know that he's still laughing. His back shudders, and She looks at me angrily.

I feel her controlling me, my will dissolving before the force of her fury. She whispers in my ear, instructing me. I repeat what she says out loud, as if the act of pronouncing the sentences would activate my body. I kneel and grasp the shovel. It's heavy. I appreciate the density of the object, the effectiveness of its mass. I plant my feet firmly, one on each side of Rockabilly. My toes sink into the mud. I focus on the base of his head. I take the shovel in both hands and raise it high above me.

I'm able to see her as I bring the steel towards his skull. Her ink squirms in delight.

BONES

On the Western horizon a storm is gathering. I can see the languid flashes of lightning from here. It's coming towards us slowly, but it's coming. At dawn, rain will fall. A spring downpour. I like the idea. We could use it.

I'm a bit restless. I leave the chimney and go up to the roof's peak. It's not easy. The tile is slippery, I can barley grip it. From this higher vantage point, I can see the edge of the suburb. The landscape looks like a scale model, like the neighborhood was really just a miniature of an already-existing place. Far away, there is Wal-Mart's glowing sign. Rising above the houses, it crowns the suburb like it were a temple or a jewel... No, even better, a radiant lighthouse that watches over us all.

I hear laughter. It's coming from Rockabilly's crater. I bark three times and go back to the chimney so I can see better. There is Rockabilly, lying face down in the dirt and not laughing anymore. He's still. Babyface is also in the hole. Naked, standing above Rockabilly. He's got an object in his hands, he raises it. The shovel's steel glints in the darkness. I get excited again. I spin, I whine, I wag my tail. I scratch at the tiles with my front paws, and butt my head against the brick chimney.

The shovel comes down with violence. I hear the noises the blow makes. The muffled wetness of the tendons, the crack of the skull, the metallic scrape of steel against bone.

Babyface is panting. He catches his breath, then raises the shovel again for a second blow.

SUICIDE GIRL

Mom's sleeping. She's unconscious. There's an empty bottle of Johnny Walker lying in her splayed fingers. I crawl over to the foot of the bed, then get to my feet in front of the TV. My shadow is cast across her body. She's still lying against the headboard, her head drooping, a string of drool wetting the collar of her bathrobe. The rest of her body is a wrapped-up bulge under the blankets. I remember how when I was little, when I was afraid of sleeping alone in the dark, I would get out of bed and run to Mom's room. It always felt like a shadow was chasing at my heels, and I would only be able to save myself if I could reach Mom's room before the darkness overtook me. I remember how she would always sleep wrapped up. Cocooned like a little girl, the covers pulled up to her eyes. I would get under the covers, and she would receive me wordlessly. Mom wouldn't wake up, but somehow her body would recognize me. She would take me in her arms, and I would take refuge under the blankets. She never rejected me. It was our secret ritual, night after night. I've never felt as protected as I did then. I miss that, I want it back. I long for that refuge, for her to shelter me in the warmth of her breast. But that woman no longer exists. She disappeared many years ago. She was replaced by a stranger, by a horrible, cruel being. She transformed into the shadow, into the darkness that was trying to hurt me. Now she barely looks like Mom. When I was a girl, her eyes shone. Her skin was radiant, and she always smelled like springtime. Not anymore. Her eyes are dull, her skin is rough, even her voice is deeper. She's not fooling anyone. Chuck always knew, hiding under his rock ,when she would come into the room. He would stay there for hours and not come out of his hiding place until the light in Mom's room went out.

From behind me, I can hear the TV's purr. They're showing an ad for Wal-Mart. Something about a new line of gas masks. There on sale on Sunday.

I lift the quilt. I can see her legs, her hands are in between her knees. I get in and wriggle under the blankets. It smells like whisky and sweat. I proceed with caution, not wanting to wake her. One of her feet scrapes my leg. The sole is calloused. I keep climbing up on top of her. I put my ear to her chest. Her breath is light; the beats are irregular. She has a gold ring hanging from a thin chain. When I was a girl, she would let me hold it and tell me to be careful. I would put it on my ring finger, like I were married. It was huge on me, it would even fall off my thumb. Mom would always help me look for it, telling me not to worry, it couldn't have gone far. She made sure that I found it, and when I did, she would praise me.

I miss you …

I kneel on the mattress, one knee on each side of her. She doesn't even move. Johnny Walker takes care of keeping her asleep. I push the hair off her forehead and comb it with my fingers. I scrutinize her face, looking for an angle, an expression—but it's no use. I close my eyes and I feel her cheeks, her lips. I picture how it used to be, when she smiled.

Without looking, I lean over and feel around the night table. I grab the telephone receiver and stretch out the cord. I open my eyes and start coiling the cable around her neck. Her chin is drooping. I push it up, so I can cinch the cord tight. Mom wets her lips but aside from that doesn't react. I touch her ears and caress her neck. I wedge a pillow behind her head so she doesn't hit it against the wood headboard. I again take her chin and gently open her mouth. I wad up the panties that I've been carrying and stuff them between her teeth. I dry her drool with the sleeve of my nightshirt and wet my thumb to smooth down her eyebrows. Through the window I can hear a dog howling. The clank of Rockabilly's shovel has been replaced by laughter. I take the cable in both hands.

Bitch.

I hold my breath and pull. Hard. I pull with all my might. I see how the cord sinks into the skin of her neck. My knuckles go white, the cable cutting off the circulation in my fingers. She raises her eyebrows, but doesn't wake up. Little by little, her face darkens. The rise and fall of her chest slows. I redouble my efforts, my body shaking. I dig my elbows into the mattress and bite my lip. I feel the metallic taste of blood pour into my mouth. My arms are burning, but I don't let up. I lean my head forward, buttressing it against the headboard. My hair brushes her face. I push my knees against the cable. Something inside her gives. Her eyes open, her pupils dilated. I can't hold back the tears any longer. I see her, finally see her. She's back.

Mom ...

I drop the cord, take her by the shoulders, and pull her to me. Her head lolls. I support it in my hands. My sobs become wails, my tears fall on her lips. Her body is free, her chest still.

Mom ...

BONES

The sound of the shovel connecting with Rockabilly's head is the only sound to be heard. The night grows tired, smells dissipating, the wind dying down. I sit back on my haunches. Something has changed. I feel a fog forming in my head, like the world were suddenly growing blurry, and the lucidity of last night were evaporating.

The sparrows are back, and they're awake now. Dawn is approaching. They're clinging to the oak's branches and have halted their song, obeying a signal only they understand. A morning mist forms on the suburb's yards. It floats on the grass and spills over the sidewalks until it sinks into the sewer grates. The asphalt is wet, the black pavement reflecting the streetlights. Far off, I can make out a cat crossing an intersection. It doesn't excite me. I don't know what's going on, but I don't even lift my head. I watch it until it disappears into the bushes of the next block. Some windows start to light up, people who wake up in the early hours, when darkness still reigns. A mailman, a police officer, a nurse. That kind of person. The ones who go to sleep early and wake up before the rest. I imagine them, sitting on the edges of their beds, rubbing their eyes, asking themselves how much longer they're going to keep taking this life, asking themselves when things are finally going to change. A few contemplate leaving it all, others get up resigned to the routine ahead, and one of them does what he has done every morning for the last eight months. He opens the drawer in the night-stand and looks at the bottle of sleeping pills. This time he goes for it. He takes the bottle and opens it.

In the distance, I can see the highway. A line of lights forms. Here are the cars of these same people. They're heading for other places—places I've never been that lie outside of the limits of my world. My owner is probably in his car, going to his place in the distance. I ask myself if there are other suburbs like this one, with streets, with houses like the ones here. Is there another dog like me, barking in some yard, or asleep on some roof, who suddenly has language and acquires the ability to think, to think for real, not like before? The fog in my head is getting thicker. Soon I will forget all of this, I will return to being an unthinking beast of instinct and feeling. I will go back to my owner, waiting for him to feed me, for him to throw a stick for me to fetch. That will be the scope of my world. Maybe it's better that way.

I return my gaze to the crater. Babyface is still standing in the hole. He's supporting himself on the shovel, panting. His back shudders, his lungs fighting to fill themselves with air. His naked body has been doused in mud, blood, and sweat.

Babyface starts swaying and whispering something. He repeats it again and again. I cock my ears, but I can't pick up any more than a murmur. It's melodic, hypnotic, barely coming from his chest, as if it were formed in some deep secret cavity, hidden in the depths of his throat. It creates a deep vibrating harmony. His breath synchs up with the rhythm. He relaxes, his arms fall slack.

I smell something burning. I can barely detect it, but it's getting stronger. It's coming from Suicide Girl's house. A window lights up. I can see how the flames lick at the walls, making the wallpaper curl. The fire strengthens, black smoke starts filtering out of the edges of the windows, and a breeze blows the haze towards Babyface. He's fixated on something else. He stops whispering, drops the shovel, and kneels down. He takes Rockabilly's corpse, grabbing it by the waist, and pulls it out of the mud. He's not strong enough to push it out of the hole, but he's able to get the torso up onto the lip, the legs hanging back down.

The blaze spreads to the rest of the house, consuming the roof. I feel the flames' heat. I like the sensation, it's pleasant. Babyface stands there, looking at Rockabilly's body. He runs a hand along his back, caressing it. He smiles and traces the ink silhouette with his finger. She's still, empty—something tells me that she's no longer there, that it's only a tattoo now. Nothing more.

I shake my head. I need to focus. I'm at a loss for words. My mind is clouding over. Not yet ... Not yet.

Some neighbors approach to watch the fire. They arrive in pajamas, in bathrobes, in slippers. They watch it in silence, their faces illuminated by the blaze. Nobody is talking, nobody goes for help. They just watch, like they were witnessing something divine. A miracle from another world. They still don't react when Suicide Girl emerges from the flames. She comes out barefoot, with her shirt unbuttoned, covered in soot. She looks lost, like she doesn't know where she is. She stumbles, taking unsure steps, trying to orient herself.

Babyface moves, distancing himself from Rockabilly's corpse. He rubs his hands over his body, trying to clean the sweat and blood off his skin. He shakes his enormous head and dries his eyes on his wrist. He breathes in.

He picks the shovel up out of the mud.

He's in the center of the crater. He looks down and plunges the steel into the ground. He digs with determination, his movements becoming fluid. Dirt flies out of the hole.

Suicide Girl approaches. The fire illuminates everything. She gets to the lip of the crater and stands there, looking at Rockabilly's body. Suicide Girl looks debilitated, she can barely hold herself up in the breeze. A few seconds later, her knees buckle, and she falls beside him. She curls up in the mud in the fetal position. I can smell her through the smoke. She smells like milk. She brings her hand to her left arm and distractedly rubs away the tattoo she had drawn there. The horizon is growing pale. The sparrows begin their song, and while the wind picks up, the raindrops start falling.

My eyes close. The night, the words … Everything slips away.

ORIGINAL SPANISH PUBLICATION:
ROCKABILLY
ALFAGUARA EDICIONES 2011
© MIKE WILSON

© DIAPHANES 2018
ISBN 978-3-0358-0097-5

DIAPHANES
HARDSTR. 69 | CH-8004 ZURICH
DRESDENER STR. 118 | D-10999 BERLIN

PRINTED IN GERMANY
LAYOUT: 2EDIT, ZURICH

WWW.DIAPHANES.COM